Freedmen's Town
Then & Now

Charonda Johnson
Priscilla T Graham

Copyright © 2021 by Freedmen's Town Association, Inc.
All Rights Reserved.
Freedmen's Town Then & Now
ISBN: 978-1-953824-03-5
Printed in the United States of America

All Rights Reserved. No part of this book may be reproduced or transmitted in any form or by any means, electronic or mechanical, including photocopying, recording or any information storage and retrieval system without written permission of the publisher except for brief quotations used in reviews, written specifically for inclusion in a newspaper, blog, or magazine.

Cover design and book layout by Priscilla T Graham

In the making of this book, every attempt has been made to verify names, facts, and figures.

Photos: Public Domain, FTA Collection, Gladys House, and Priscilla T Graham

Written by Charonda Johnson and Priscilla T Graham

Dedicated to the great men and women who built and settled Houston Historic Freedmen's Town. Their perseverance and accomplishments deserve recognition and celebration! African American History is American History.

Content

Freedmen's Town	6
Gladys House	8
Crossroads	13
Matthews Street	14
Bailey Street	18
Saulnier Street	20
Robin Street	30
Andrews Street	36
Cleveland Street	72
Ruthven Street	76
Wilson Street	78
Victor	80
West Gray	90
Allen Parkway	92
Valentines	94
Taft Street	100
Ruthven Street	102
West Dallas	110
Lamb Street	112

Freedmen's Town

Immediately west of downtown Houston lies the city's oldest Indigenous African American community affectionately known as Historic Freedmen's Town located in Fourth Ward. Wards were established in 1841. Although the *ward system* was officially discontinued in 1906, Houstonians continued to identify the city's various communities by those political subdivisions.

Freedmen's Town was established immediately after the Civil War on the southern banks of Buffalo Bayou in 1865 across the street from where The Historic Oaks of Allen Parkway stands today. During the turn of the century, Freedmen's Town was a thriving, prosperous, and self-sufficient community. Economic, community, and social development were at its peak.

Freedmen's Town boundaries once extended east to Travis Street; west to Taft Street; north to Allen Parkway, and from Buffalo Bayou south to Sutton Street. It encompassed most of what is now downtown Houston west of Main Street, as well as the residential areas along San Felipe Street (now West Dallas) and West Gray.

By the early twentieth century, Freedmen's Town housed prominent educational institutions and most of the African American physicians and attorneys, while at night its bars and night spots attracted whites and blacks who came to hear great blues and jazz musicians.

The most common types of residential housing by 1907 were T and L shaped houses and several two-story tenements. Commercial buildings, churches, and schools were built along major streets and commercial buildings, cafes, grocery stores, or bars were usually built on the corner of residential blocks.

Over the years eminent domain laws, encroachment, constriction of interstate 45, and Historic Oaks of Allen Parkway Village along with unexplained fires, inappropriate alterations, and demolitions of historic structures have destroyed the geographical integrity of the community.

In 1985, Freedmen's Town was designated as a historic district in the National Register of Historic Places. At that time, 568 historic structures stood in the 40 block area. Today, most of the historic structures have been destroyed and about seven-tenth of a mile of the original brick streets remain. Freedmen's Town Then & Now is the community's response to ensure that we celebrate and remember the lives of those who lived, worshiped, and walked the streets of Historic Freedmen's Town in Houston's 4th Ward, Texas.

Gladys Marie House

Gladys Marie House is a native Houstonian and owner of Affordable Carpets, LLC. She is a longtime Fourth Ward Freedmen's Town activist who was born and grew up in Houston's Historic Freedmen's Town. House researched the history of Freedman's Town via oral interviews and archival data; co-founded Freedmen's Town Association, Inc. in 1980, and obtained its legal status on March 16, 1981 in order to preserve and restore the oldest African American neighborhood in Houston dating to 1845.

In 1984, the Freedmen's Town Association applied for and received a grant from the National Trust for historic preservation to conduct a historic site survey of the community. House worked tirelessly to document and house legitimate history of Freedman's Town in the Julia Ideson Library. She submitted a nomination for designation of the community as a National Historic Site ; however, only 40 of the original 80 sites received the designation in 1985 as a historic district in the National Register of Historic Places.

House developed the Freedmen's Town Redevelopment Plan in 1995 as the guide to revitalization of the neighborhood and empowerment of the longtime grass root residents. She used her social, housing, and economic development skills to train and develop non-profit board members, volunteers, committees, and various program participants. House also worked with Mexican residents in obtaining affordable housing, assistance, employment, health care, and general social services. She designed the first winged panty napkin in June 1984, but patent was not obtained and despite the product having had been rejected by Proctor & Gamble and other such companies, the winged napkin hit the market a year later.

Freedmen's Town Association, Inc. (FTA)
Mission
- To preserve and restore the Freedmen's Town community and empower the residents of Freedmen's Town.
- To serve as an advocate for affordable housing and economic development in Freedmen's Town.

Belief
Fundamental to FTA's mission, is the organization's belief in a grass-roots community controlled approach to community and economic development.

Promise
- FTA will be accountable to the low and moderate income community it serves.
- FTA will be committed to integrity in community building and revitalization.
- FTA will help residents build ownership of physical and monetary assets in order to escape from poverty.
- FTA will spearhead the building of indigenous leadership in the Freedmen's Town community.
- FTA will use the latest technology to inform, educate, and inspire the Freedmen's Town community to participate in the revitalization of their community.

Freedmen's Town Association, Inc. (developer and builder) broke ground on March 18, 1999 at 10:30 am in the 1300 block of Saulnier Street to provide affordable housing for low to moderate working class families. Each of the new two story homes are 1,670 square feet, 3

bedroom, 1.5 baths, and garage. Freedmen's Town Association, Inc. built a total of four homes and rehabbed 14 others.

Freedmen's Town Association opened Camp Logan Sandwich Shop located at 1015 1/2 West Dallas Street on Friday, August 17, 1990.

Crossroads 1300 Andrews and 1300 Wilson

1100 Matthews Street

1300 Matthews Street

1207 Bailey Street

707 Saulnier Street

1419 Saulnier Street (westside)

1519 Saulnier Street

1600 Saulnier Street (rear)

1601 Saulnier Street (rear)

1320 Robin Street

1200 Gillette and 1500 Robin Street

1508 Robin Street

817 Andrews Street

816 Andrews Street

818 Andrews Street

800 -830 Andrews Street (even numbers)

800 -830 Andrews Street (even numbers)

820 Andrews Street

1200 Andrews and 1300 Cushing Street

1207 Andrews Street

1208 Andrews Street

1209 Andrews Street

1210 Andrews Street

1211 Andrews Street

1314 Andrews Street

1415 Andrews Street

1500 Andrews and 1200 Bailey

1500 Andrews Street

1501 Andrews Street

1518 Andrews Street

1600 Andrews Street

1700 Andrews Street

1204 Cleveland Street

1206 Cleveland Street

1208 Cleveland Street

1210 Cleveland Street

1612 Ruthven

1116 Wilson Street

1300 Victor Street

1500 Victor Street

1208 Victor Street

1206 Victor Street

1204 Victor Street

138 West Gray

1801 Allen Parkway

1408 Valentines Street

1106 Valentines Street

1407 Valentines Street

1101 Taft Street

1104 Ruthven Street

1406 Ruthven Street

1606 Ruthven Street

1612 Ruthven Street

907 W Dallas Street

900 Lamb Street and 1300 W Dallas Street

www.ingramcontent.com/pod-product-compliance
Lightning Source LLC
Chambersburg PA
CBHW040730250426
43671CB00032B/23